Original title:
Past the Hurt

Copyright © 2024 Swan Charm
All rights reserved.

Author: Paulina Pähkel
ISBN HARDBACK: 978-9916-89-853-6
ISBN PAPERBACK: 978-9916-89-854-3
ISBN EBOOK: 978-9916-89-855-0

# **Chronicles of Resilience**

In the shadowed valley, we tread,
Guided by faith, our spirits fed.
With every trial, we rise anew,
Strength entwined with hope so true.

Through storms that rage and winds that howl,
A light within us, a sacred prowl.
With hearts afire, we carry on,
Through darkest nights, we seek the dawn.

In silence deep, we find our voice,
In faith we stand, in love rejoice.
Our journey long, yet spirits soar,
In every loss, we gain much more.

Hand in hand, united we stand,
With grace bestowed, we understand.
Resilience blooms in barren ground,
In every tear, new joys are found.

For in this life, we bear the weight,
Yet rise again, to love, not hate.
Each step a testament, bold and bright,
Chronicles written in pure light.

## Testaments of the Spirit

Whispers of the ancients call,
In sacred verses, we stand tall.
With words like petals, soft and sweet,
We gather strength in quiet retreat.

Each prayer lifted to the sky,
A testament that we will fly.
In unity, our voices blend,
A chorus strong that will not end.

Our hearts aflame with purpose clear,
In trials faced, we shed a tear.
Yet from the ashes, hope does rise,
The spirit dances, breaks the ties.

Through mountains high and valleys low,
We find the paths that help us grow.
In every heartbeat, faith's embrace,
In love eternal, we find grace.

So let us walk this road with pride,
Together still, we will abide.
Testaments of spirit, soar above,
In every challenge, we find love.

## The Sanctuary of Tomorrow

In quiet whispers, hope does rise,
A sanctuary built in the skies.
With faith as our guide, we'll tread this way,
Tomorrow's light will break the gray.

Here in this haven, love's embrace,
We find our strength, our sacred space.
With open hearts, we'll boldly stand,
In tomorrow's dreams, united hand in hand.

**From Ashes to Altar**

From ashes cold, new life does spring,
An altar built with the songs we sing.
Through trials faced, we rise anew,
Transformed and whole, in love so true.

Each tear we shed, a seed of grace,
In every wound, the light we trace.
From sorrow's depth, we take our flight,
To serve the world by love's pure light.

## **A Pilgrimage Through Pain**

On this path, with burdens worn,
We walk with faith, though hearts be torn.
With every step, our purpose clear,
In pain we find what we hold dear.

Each stumble tells a tale of gain,
A journey lit by love through pain.
The spirit guides, through darkest night,
A pilgrim's heart shall find the light.

## **The Garden of Forgiveness**

In tender space, where shadows blend,
The garden blooms, where hearts can mend.
With every seed of grace we sow,
In forgiveness, our spirits grow.

Each flower bright, a tale of peace,
In love's embrace, our doubts cease.
We walk this path, hand in hand,
In the garden's heart, forever stand.

# Sacred Threads of Life

In the loom of divine design,
We find our paths intertwined,
Each thread a prayer, a wish,
A tapestry of love aligned.

Frayed edges speak of trials,
Yet strength in every seam,
We are stitched by grace's hand,
In faith, we dare to dream.

Colors vibrant, soft and bright,
Adorn our days with light,
Through every storm, we stand tall,
Guided by His sacred might.

From ashes rise our souls anew,
Crafted by the hands of fate,
May we cherish every thread,
In gratitude, we await.

Life's fabric weaves both joy and pain,
Yet love's embrace is ever clear,
We are bound by sacred ties,
In unity, we have no fear.

## **In the Embrace of Grace**

Beneath the heavens' gentle sigh,
We find solace, hearts uplift,
In the arms of grace we lie,
Life's burdens are a sacred gift.

Each moment, tenderly bestowed,
Whispers of love softly speak,
Through trials, we find the road,
In grace, we find our strength, not weak.

With open hearts, we gather near,
In the light of truth, we stand,
United by faith, free of fear,
A family woven hand in hand.

Joy spills forth like morning dew,
Refresh our souls, renew our sight,
In the embrace of grace, we view,
The beauty of His endless light.

In laughter and in whispered prayer,
Together we create our song,
In the embrace of grace, we share,
A journey where we all belong.

**Streams of Serenity**

In quietude, the waters flow,
A balm to soothe the weary soul,
Ebbing gently, love will grow,
In streams of peace, we are made whole.

Reflecting skies of vibrant hue,
The currents sing of hope, of dreams,
Each ripple whispers, pure and true,
In faith's embrace, our spirit beams.

Amidst the chaos, find your calm,
Let burdens drift upon the breeze,
In stillness, find the sacred psalm,
Where heart and spirit find their ease.

The shore calls gently, beckons near,
A witness to our sacred ties,
In every drop, a promise clear,
To rise again, beneath the skies.

So come, partake in nature's grace,
Where every sound invites us home,
In streams of serenity, we trace,
The journey's end, in love we roam.

## **The Anointing of Hope**

In the stillness of the night,
Anoint us with thy sacred balm,
With faith's gentle guiding light,
In despair, we find our calm.

Hope flows like oil on our skin,
A reminder of love divine,
In our hearts, let it begin,
To heal the wounds, our spirits shine.

Lifted high above our fears,
The anointing grace surrounds,
Through laughter, joy, and silent tears,
A symphony of life's sweet sounds.

In every moment, seek and find,
The blessing that we hold so dear,
Anoint us, Lord, with heart and mind,
In love's embrace, we conquer fear.

As dawn breaks clear, the world awakes,
With hope, renewed, we walk in faith,
The anointing love we partake,
Forever held in grace's wraith.

## The Altar of Healing

On the altar of healing, souls renew,
With whispered prayers, the spirit's view.
Each tear a seed, in sacred ground,
From brokenness, strength is found.

Hands raised high, seeking the light,
In darkness, faith ignites the night.
Hearts entwined in divine embrace,
Restoration flows, a holy grace.

The past may linger, but hope is near,
In every heartbeat, love draws near.
A gentle touch, a fervent plea,
Bringing forth the soul's decree.

With each breath, the journey grows,
In sacred silence, the spirit glows.
Through pain, a purpose, love shall flow,
The altar of healing, hearts aglow.

## Serene Waters of Grace

By serene waters, spirits find peace,
In quiet ripples, all worries cease.
With every drop, a blessing flows,
In tranquil depths, true love grows.

The stillness whispers ancient truths,
In nature's arms, eternal youths.
Beneath the surface, treasures lie,
In moments shared, we touch the sky.

The sun sets lightly, casting gold,
In this haven, hearts unfold.
With faith's embrace, fears take flight,
In the waters, we find our light.

Here time dissolves, the world fades fast,
In reverence, present and past.
Together we gather, hand in hand,
By serene waters, we take our stand.

## Cloaked in Faith

Cloaked in faith, I walk the path,
Through trials fierce, through shadows' wrath.
With each step, a prayer released,
In sacred trust, my soul finds peace.

Though storms may rise and darkness call,
In faith's embrace, I shall not fall.
The voice of hope within me sings,
Through every tempest, joy it brings.

With courage bound in love's sweet light,
I rise once more, embracing the fight.
Each setback, a lesson, I grow strong,
Cloaked in faith, where I belong.

The world around may twist and turn,
But in my heart, the flame shall burn.
In unity with those who seek,
Cloaked in faith, their strength I speak.

**The Weight of Sorrow**

The weight of sorrow rests like stone,
In the quiet, I feel alone.
With heavy hearts, we search for grace,
In shadows cast, we find our place.

Yet in the darkness, love shines bright,
A beacon calls us to the light.
Each tear a testament of strength,
In every sorrow, a lengthened length.

As burdens shift with every breath,
We turn to faith, defying death.
In shared embrace, a solace found,
Together we rise from broken ground.

Through grief we learn and grow anew,
Finding beauty in the blue.
With open hearts, we shall explore,
The weight of sorrow, we bear no more.

## Petals on Sacred Grounds

On hallowed earth the petals lay,
A whisper soft of dawn's array.
In gentle prayer, our spirits rise,
To greet the sun in painted skies.

With every step, a grace we tread,
In unity, where hearts are led.
The fragrance sweet of hope and love,
Unfolds the truth that's sent from above.

Beneath the trees where shadows sway,
The roots of faith hold night and day.
In silence deep, the echoes breathe,
A truth that binds, a web it weaves.

The petals dance in holy breeze,
A sacred hymn that brings us peace.
With reverence, we bow our heads,
And trace the paths where spirit spreads.

In sacred grounds, our souls ignite,
With every bond, we share the light.
These petals paved, in grace we stand,
Together strong, in holy land.

## **Threads of the Infinite**

In the loom of time, we weave our fates,
Threads entwined, where love creates.
Each strand a story, luminous, bright,
Guided by an unseen light.

From darkness springs the dawn of grace,
In every challenge, we find our place.
The tapestry, a sacred art,
It binds us all, play every part.

With threads of hope, we stitch anew,
The infinite forms both old and true.
In faith we trust, as we embark,
To light the world, ignite the spark.

Interwoven dreams, forever dance,
In the heart's rhythm, a holy chance.
Embracing love, we break the chains,
In unity, where joy remains.

Threads of the infinite, strong yet fine,
In every pulse, the sacred sign.
Together we weave, together we pray,
In the fabric of life, we find our way.

## Relics of Faith

In ancient halls where shadows dwell,
Relics whisper tales to tell.
Each token worn, a sacred trust,
In every heart, a hidden gust.

The faith of ages, we hold tight,
In darkest days, it shines so bright.
These relics forged in trials face,
A testament of love and grace.

With grateful hands, we raise our voice,
In unity, we make the choice.
To honor paths our ancestors tread,
The living truth in words unsaid.

Through storms and trials, we shall stand,
With relics close, we join our hand.
In every tear, a lesson lies,
With every joy, the spirit flies.

Relics of faith, protecting souls,
In timeless light, the spirit rolls.
Together we stand, a chain unbroken,
In love and hope, our hearts are spoken.

## **Emblems of Grace**

In gentle light, the emblems shine,
A divine dance of the sacred line.
In every heart, love finds its place,
A beacon bright, the gift of grace.

With open arms, we hold the truth,
A child's laughter, the joy of youth.
In kindness shared, in moments small,
The emblems lift us, one and all.

Through trials faced, through paths unknown,
The grace we seek, in prayer is sown.
In every breath, the spirit flows,
With every act, compassion grows.

Emblems of grace, a guiding star,
They light the way, no matter how far.
In unity, we stand as one,
In every journey, the will is done.

In the sacred script, it's clearly seen,
That grace transforms, like a silver sheen.
In love and faith, we find our place,
Together, blessed, by emblems of grace.

## **The Return to Wholeness**

In silence we seek the guiding light,
Hearts open wide, embracing the night.
With hands uplifted, we call His name,
Restoring our souls, no longer the same.

Through trials and storms, our spirits rise,
In faith we find strength, the truth never lies.
With every step taken, on paths made new,
In Him we are whole, our spirits renew.

The journey of grace, a sacred dance,
In His love we are held, a holy romance.
Forgiveness bestowed, our burdens released,
In His tender mercy, we find our peace.

So let us rejoice in this blessed embrace,
In the arms of His love, we find our place.
Each moment a gift, in His presence we stand,
Together in wholeness, hand in hand.

## **Journey Through the Wilderness**

In shadowed valleys, where heartaches roam,
We wander in search of a place called home.
With every footstep, in faith we tread,
Guided by whispers, where angels have led.

The sun may be hidden, the night may be long,
Yet still hope arises, in spirit we're strong.
For rivers shall flow, where deserts once were,
In the midst of the struggle, His promises stir.

Each trial a lesson, each heartache a grace,
We find in the journey, our sacred space.
Through thorns and through thistles, we rise above,
In the wilderness, we are cradled by love.

So let courage guide us through treacherous lands,
For He walks beside us, with outstretched hands.
In the wilderness vast, new paths we will see,
With faith as our compass, forever we're free.

**Candles in the Darkness**

In the hush of the night, candles softly glow,
Whispers of hope in the shadows below.
Each flame a reminder, that light will prevail,
In the heart of the darkness, love will not fail.

When troubles surround us, and fears come to call,
Let us light our candles, together stand tall.
For in unity's warmth, we find strength anew,
Guided by faith, we find courage true.

Every flicker of light, a prayer to the skies,
In moments of doubt, our spirits will rise.
Together we kindle, this sacred embrace,
A beacon of love, in the great human race.

So hold your candle high, let the light shine bright,
In the yearning for peace, dispel every fright.
Through trials and darkness, we'll always abide,
In the arms of His love, forever our guide.

## Songs of the Redeemed

In the morning light, we raise our song,
Voices united, together we belong.
With hearts set ablaze, we sing out with cheer,
The songs of the redeemed, for heaven is near.

From shadows of doubt, our spirits take flight,
In the warmth of His love, we bask in the light.
Each note tells a story, each melody free,
A testament joyful, of what we can be.

With every refrain, we break every chain,
In the chorus of grace, eternally gain.
For we are the cherished, the lost now found,
In the songs of the faithful, redemption resounds.

So let the bells ring, let the heavens sing,
In the journey of life, our praises we bring.
With hope as our anthem, we rise and we soar,
In the songs of the redeemed, forever restore.

## A Chorus of Resounding Hope

In the silence of the night,
A gentle whisper starts to rise.
Hearts together, pure and bright,
In faith, the soul never dies.

Each step we take in trust and grace,
Guided by a light divine.
In every challenge, we embrace,
A chorus, steadfast and benign.

From valleys deep, to mountains high,
We gather strength from every tear.
With open hearts, we lift our sigh,
In unity, we conquer fear.

The dawn will break, the shadows fade,
With every promise, love is sown.
Through trials faced, a path is laid,
In harmony, we're never alone.

In this life, in love's refrain,
Hope resounds like sacred song.
Through storms and peace, through joy and pain,
In faith united, we belong.

## In the Light of Forgiveness


Oh, let the light of grace unfold,
To heal the wounds we bear inside.
In tender moments, stories told,
Forgiveness blooms where love abides.

With every breath, a chance to mend,
The broken ties that time has frayed.
In humble hearts, we find a friend,
In faith, our burdens softly laid.

Each gentle word, a balm to save,
Transcending pain, and doubt, and fear.
In mercy's arms, the lost can brave,
The shadows fade when love draws near.

When wrongs are righted, peace will reign,
A sacred bond, renewed in trust.
Our spirits lifted, healed from pain,
In grace, we rise from earthly dust.

So let us walk this path of light,
With open hearts that freely share.
In every joy, in every plight,
Forgiveness dwells, our souls laid bare.

## **Grace in the Shadows**

In the depths where shadows play,
A flicker of grace begins to gleam.
In quiet sighs, we find the way,
A glimmering thread of hope we dream.

Through trials faced, we search for light,
The gentle whispers guide our hearts.
In darkest hours, we find our might,
Grace fills the void, never departs.

Each storm we weather leads us near,
To truths that shimmer through the pain.
In every tear, a lesson dear,
Through sorrows, joy will bloom again.

With every step and every fall,
We rise with faith, our spirits soar.
In love's embrace, we heed the call,
Grace in the shadows, forevermore.

Held by the light that transcends time,
In every struggle, hope will grow.
Our lives a poem, a sacred rhyme,
Grace in the shadows, forever glow.

## **Resurrection of the Soul**

In silence deep, a promise stirs,
A seed of life breaks through the clay.
From depths of grief, a hope occurs,
Resurrection calls, lighting the way.

Through trials faced, we learn to rise,
With every heartbeat, life reborn.
In love, we shed our earthly ties,
A new horizon, bright with dawn.

From ashes warm, a spirit flies,
In faith's embrace, we find our role.
Each tear that falls, each heartfelt sigh,
Ignites the fire, resurrects the soul.

Through death's cold grasp, we fight to stand,
With open arms, we greet the light.
In unity, we make our stand,
In love's embrace, we end the night.

So let us sing of life's delight,
With every breath, the world we know.
In resurrection's sacred light,
The soul awakens, love will flow.

## **Bridges Built in Silence**

In quietude, the heart does sing,
Connecting souls with gentle strings.
Between the shadows, light will weave,
A sacred bond for those who believe.

With love as glue, our spirits soar,
Embracing peace forevermore.
In whispered prayers, we find our way,
Building bridges day by day.

Silence speaks where words may fail,
A testament of faith we hail.
In stillness, strength begins to rise,
As hearts transform beneath the skies.

With every step upon this ground,
In sacred trust, together bound.
We journey forth, hand in hand,
United by a love so grand.

So let us tread this path of grace,
With open hearts, we find our place.
Through silent bridges, we unite,
In harmony, we share the light.

## **The Alchemy of Suffering**

In trials deep, our spirits yearn,
From ashes, hope we slowly burn.
The furnace of our darkest hour,
Transforms our pain into divine power.

Each drop of tear, a seed of faith,
In struggles, grace begins to bathe.
For every wound, a lesson learned,
In suffering, our hearts are turned.

With each heartache, wisdom grows,
In shadows cast, the light still glows.
Through tempest's roar, we stand our ground,
In the silence, strength is found.

In breaking, we are made anew,
The spirit's fire, relentless and true.
Alchemy, a sacred art,
Transforms our grief, ignites the heart.

So let us rise through every storm,
Embracing change, we start to form.
In the alchemy of life's embrace,
We find our peace, our holy space.

## **The Resurrection of Hope**

In the stillness of the night,
When shadows loom, and faith takes flight.
A whisper calls, a soft embrace,
As hope is born in darkest place.

From barren ground, the flowers bloom,
With colors bright, dispelling gloom.
Each petal soft, a promise made,
In the resurrection, fears do fade.

As dawn breaks through the heavy veil,
The heart's refrain, a fervent tale.
In every breath, a prayer we find,
In hope, our spirits intertwined.

Through trials faced, we learn to stand,
With faith and love, we hold His hand.
For every loss, a new beginning,
The resurrection of hope is winning.

So in the light, let our voices rise,
In unity, we reach for skies.
In every heart, let hope ignite,
A beacon shining, pure and bright.

## **In Prayer We Rise**

In sacred moments, hearts align,
With whispered prayers, the soul will shine.
In unity, we find our strength,
In prayer, we travel any length.

Each word a vessel, carrying dreams,
Together, we weave our holy seams.
In humble trust, our spirits soar,
As faith embraces, we seek more.

Through trials faced, we lift our voice,
In prayerful echoes, we rejoice.
With open hearts, we share the load,
In every prayer, a sacred ode.

From valleys low to mountains high,
In every tear, a hopeful sigh.
In fellowship, we rise above,
In prayer, we find our truest love.

So let our words like incense rise,
In gratitude, beneath the skies.
In prayer, we find our wings to fly,
Uniting souls, we cannot die.

**Arriving at the Horizon**

Upon the morn, when dawn unveils,
A promise whispers through the gales.
With faith we travel, hearts aligned,
To seek the truth that light has signed.

The path we walk is rich with grace,
Divine embrace in every space.
Through shadows deep, we find our way,
A guiding hand that will not sway.

Each step we take, a prayer we breathe,
In nature's book, our souls bequeath.
The horizon calls, bright dreams await,
In sacred time, we contemplate.

In silence found, the spirit sings,
Of love and hope, and all such things.
The journey's end, a sacred height,
In every heart, the holy light.

With arms outstretched towards the sky,
We celebrate, no need to sigh.
Together bound, in joy we rise,
Arriving where the spirit flies.

## The Splendor of Grace

In quiet moments, grace descends,
A gentle touch that never ends.
Through trials faced, we hold the light,
In splendor wrapped, our hearts take flight.

Each tear we shed, a sacred call,
To rise anew, to stand, not fall.
The grace revealed in every plight,
Transforms our darkness into light.

With open hands, we share the load,
The burden lightens on this road.
In every heart, a story told,
Of love unearned, and faith so bold.

The splendor blooms in kindness shared,
A beacon bright for the prepared.
In unity, our voices blend,
Transforming strangers into friends.

When shadows loom and doubts confide,
In grace, we stand, our fears subside.
Together in this dance of grace,
We find our place in love's embrace.

# Light Shines from Within

Deep in the soul, a flame does glow,
A sacred light, our hearts bestow.
In quiet whispers, truth be told,
The essence pure, more precious than gold.

Through storms we face, the light remains,
A steadfast course through joy and pains.
In darkest nights, its warmth we find,
A beacon bright, our hearts aligned.

Each moment shared, a ripple flows,
The light within, a garden grows.
In selfless love, we shine together,
A tapestry of faith, a tether.

When doubts entangle, spirits fray,
The inner light will lead the way.
In every breath, let hope begin,
For true love's flame shines bright within.

As morning breaks and shadows flee,
We find our strength in purity.
With love as guide, our spirits spin,
In all we do, light shines within.

## Seasons of Renewal

In autumn's chill, the leaves descend,
A cycle marked, where time must bend.
Each season speaks in whispers soft,
Of life reborn, and spirits aloft.

In winter's grasp, the silence grows,
A sacred pause, where stillness flows.
Yet in the dark, a spark ignites,
Of rebirth's promise, new delights.

With spring's embrace, the blossoms wake,
In vibrant hues, our hearts shall take.
A song of hope, in every bloom,
A testament that finds its room.

Through summers long, we gather light,
In laughter shared, our souls take flight.
We dance with joy in fields of grace,
In every moment, we find our place.

These seasons mark the soul's own flight,
In every change, there shines a light.
In cycles grand, both soft and true,
We blossom bright, in all we do.

## Beneath the Shadow of the Almighty

In twilight stillness, we find our peace,
Beneath His wings, our burdens cease.
The whisper of grace, a gentle call,
In His embrace, we stand tall.

The mountains bow, the oceans still,
In every heart, His love does fill.
Through stormy nights and brightest days,
We walk in trust, endless praise.

His light guides us, a path so bright,
Each step we take, led by His might.
In quiet moments, we hear Him speak,
A sacred language, strong yet meek.

With every trial, His hand we cling,
In His presence, we rise and sing.
Beneath the shadow, we find our rest,
In faith, forever, we are blessed.

## The Silent Song of Healing

In the still night, whispers softly flow,
Healing hearts with love's warm glow.
Each breath we take, a sacred prayer,
In silence, we find the answered care.

The wounds of life are soothed with grace,
In the quiet, we find our place.
From sorrow's depths, the spirit sings,
A melody of hope, on gentle wings.

We gather strength from each shared tear,
In unity, we draw Him near.
For in our struggles, His light breaks through,
A silent song, forever true.

Each moment cherished, each pain embraced,
Through trials we walk, His love is traced.
In the hush of night, our spirits soar,
The silent song, forevermore.

## A Dance with the Divine

In every heartbeat, a rhythm divine,
We sway as one, His love intertwines.
With joyful steps, we trace His grace,
In this holy dance, we find our place.

The stars above join in the praise,
As we move in light, our spirits blaze.
With arms wide open, we spin and twirl,
In His presence, we are unfurled.

Each moment shared, a sacred song,
In unity, we all belong.
Through trials faced, His hand we hold,
In this dance of faith, our souls unfold.

As dawn awakens, our spirits rise,
With every step, we touch the skies.
A dance with the Divine, forever we'll sway,
In love's embrace, we find our way.

## **Reverence in the Aftermath**

In shadows deep, our hearts become,
A sacred space where light will hum.
Through trials faced, we stand as one,
In reverence born, our souls have won.

The echoes linger, a gentle grace,
In every heart, we find His face.
With hands held high, we offer prayer,
In the aftermath, His love is there.

From ashes rise, new dreams take flight,
In unity, we cultivate light.
Through storms we've weathered, we carry on,
In hope reborn, we greet the dawn.

In stillness found, our spirits heal,
With each heartbeat, His truth we feel.
In reverence deep, we trust His way,
Through every trial, we choose to stay.

## **When Wounds Become Wisdom**

In shadows deep, the heart does cry,
Yet through the tears, the spirit flies.
From broken paths, new journeys start,
Wisdom blooms where once was hurt.

Each scar a tale of battles fought,
In silence forged, the lessons taught.
Beneath the ache, a light shall gleam,
Wounds that heal can birth a dream.

The pain we bear ignites the soul,
Transforming grief, making us whole.
In every loss, a chance to find,
The strength within, the peace of mind.

With each embrace of fate's cruel hand,
We learn to rise, we learn to stand.
Compassion grows from roots of strife,
As wounds become the seeds of life.

Let not despair cloud your view,
For wisdom waits in skies so blue.
When wounds become our guiding star,
We'll find our way, no matter how far.

## The Quiet Strength of Surrender

In tranquil whispers, hearts do yield,
To forces greater, truth revealed.
A calm resolve in tangled tide,
The sacred choice to turn and bide.

With every sigh, we let go tight,
And trust the journey into the night.
In stillness, grace begins to flow,
A quiet strength in letting go.

The world may roar, the storms may rage,
Yet peace resides on every page.
In surrender, we find our wings,
Embracing all that living brings.

Faith, a gentle hand in hand,
Guides the weary to solid land.
Within the void, a life abounds,
In yielding, love comes softly 'round.

So breathe, dear soul, and rest awhile,
Your spirit blooms, your heart may smile.
In quiet strength, our hearts may learn,
The beauty found in each return.

## **The Eternal Embrace of Forgiveness**

In the depth of pain, we learn to see,
The light of hope, the chance to be.
Let grudges fade like whispers lost,
Forgiveness comes, no matter the cost.

Each heart that's bruised bears wounds unseen,
Yet through the fissures, we grow serene.
With open arms, we let love flow,
Forgiveness, a river that longs to glow.

To free the shackles of bitter strife,
We must embrace the gift of life.
An eternal bond, beyond the wrong,
In healing, we find where we belong.

Though storms may clash, and tempests roar,
Forgiveness opens every door.
A tender touch, a soothing balm,
In unity, we find our calm.

So let us rise, hand in hand,
To weave a tale in love's great band.
With each embrace, the world transforms,
In forgiveness, grace is born.

## **Finding Joy in the Ruins**

In shattered dreams where ashes lay,
A spark of hope begins to sway.
Amidst the wreckage, life will bloom,
In every corner, joy finds room.

With weary hearts, we build anew,
From broken pieces, we craft what's true.
In every crack, a story sings,
A melody of what love brings.

The path may twist, the night may fall,
Yet light emerges through it all.
In ruins bleak, we carve our grace,
Embracing life in every space.

Through trials faced, we come alive,
Finding strength and love to thrive.
From rubble raised, our spirits soar,
In every challenge, we'll find more.

So let us dance in life's embrace,
With open hearts, we'll find our place.
In every ruin, joy shall rise,
A testament beneath the skies.

## Lighthouses of Composure

In the tempest of the night, we stand,
With guiding lights, our spirits grand.
Each beam a prayer, each wave a sigh,
A tranquil heart beneath the sky.

Whispers of wisdom from shores afar,
Illuminate paths like a steadfast star.
In silence we gather, in faith we trust,
A sanctuary built from love and rust.

When shadows loom and doubts arise,
Let us find solace in silent cries.
Our lighthouses shine, unyielding and bright,
Holding us close through the depths of night.

Through storms we rise, together we stand,
With hope entwined, hand in hand.
In the heart's embrace, we find our way,
Dancing with grace as we greet the day.

## A Requiem of the Heart

In the stillness of dusk, shadows blend,
We gather our sorrows, our wounds to mend.
With echoes of love, our spirits soar,
A requiem sung for those we adore.

In the tapestry woven of laughter and tears,
We honor the moments, the hopes and fears.
May every heartbeat whisper a prayer,
In the quiet embrace of the evening air.

For the souls that departed, we light a flame,
In memories cherished, they'll never be the same.
Our hearts may ache, yet still they sing,
A song of remembrance, in joy we bring.

The chords of our love shall not fade away,
As we walk through the night, to the break of day.
Together we'll dance, in the spirit's delight,
In the cycle of life, we find our light.

## Radiance From Within

From the depths of our souls, a radiance shines,
An inner glow that transcends the lines.
It flickers and dances, a beacon of grace,
Illuminating paths that time can't erase.

In the labyrinth of thoughts, it guides us clear,
A soft whisper urging, 'Do not fear.'
With every heartbeat, we grow and learn,
In the warmth of love, our spirits burn.

With arms wide open, we embrace the day,
Grateful and humble, we find our way.
Through trials and joys, the radiance stays,
A light from within that forever plays.

As the sun rises high, casting shadows away,
We walk hand in hand, come what may.
Each moment a treasure, each breath a hymn,
In the dance of existence, forever we swim.

## Wings Unfurled

With wings unfurled, we take to the skies,
Embracing the heavens, where the spirit flies.
In freedom we soar, on whispers of grace,
A sacred journey through time and space.

In the embrace of the wind, we learn to trust,
Our hearts sing boldly, transforming dust.
Through shadows and light, we rise and glide,
In the arms of the universe, we bide.

Each feather a story of battles won,
We carry the light of the morning sun.
Together we sing, in unison bright,
Wings intertwined in the glow of the night.

With faith as our anchor, we travel far,
Captured by wonder, beneath every star.
In the dance of creation, eternally swirled,
In the sacred space, our wings unfurled.

## Traces of the Divine

In every whisper of the breeze,
The echoes of a sacred plea.
In shadows where the sunlight weaves,
A presence felt, unseen to see.

The dew on grass, a morning's gift,
A moment paused, a heart's swift lift.
In gentle rain, the earth does sigh,
A reminder of the love on high.

In laughter shared, in tears we shed,
The traces of the One who bled.
Each star that twinkles in the night,
Bears witness to a source of light.

In sacred texts, the truths unfold,
Ancient wisdom, stories told.
In every soul, a spark divine,
In seeking heart, the stars align.

With every step upon this ground,
The echoes of His grace abound.
In silence deep, in joy, in pain,
His love remains, forever plain.

## The Light After the Trial

Through valleys dark, the journey long,
In trials faced, we find the song.
Each burden borne, each tear that falls,
A prelude to the light that calls.

The woven path, though worn and frail,
Leads to the dawn where hope prevails.
In shattered dreams, the spirit learns,
Towards brighter ways, the heart still yearns.

With every storm that tests our faith,
A strength ignites, a holy wraith.
For every night that feels like pain,
The light returns, the spirit gains.

In whispered prayers, the solace found,
In every heartbeat, love surrounds.
The light after trials softly glows,
In every soul, the wisdom grows.

So trust the journey, every part,
For from the ashes, springs the heart.
In every loss, a path will bloom,
To guide us forth beyond the gloom.

## Streams of Tranquility

In stillness, find the sacred stream,
A flow of peace, a gentle dream.
Where worries fade like morning mist,
And quietude cannot resist.

The rustling leaves, a soothing song,
In nature's arms, we all belong.
Cool waters teach the heart to rest,
In tranquil moments, souls are blessed.

With every breath, the calm descends,
As love and grace, this world transcends.
In deep reflection, spirits rise,
The streams of life, where heart complies.

In solitude, the heart finds grace,
A sacred mirror, truth we face.
In mindful steps, we walk the way,
In peace, our souls will gently sway.

So seek the streams, the tranquil flow,
In every heart, let wisdom grow.
Amidst the noise, be still, be free,
Embrace the depths of serenity.

## In the Stillness We Heal

In quiet moments, healing starts,
When silence speaks, it mends the hearts.
In shadows cast by doubt and fear,
The light emerges, crystal clear.

With every pause, we breathe anew,
In stillness lies a sacred view.
The world may rush, yet here we stand,
In calm repose, we find the hand.

In gentle whispers, love is found,
The depth of grace, a sacred sound.
Each moment spent in quiet grace,
Allows the wounds to find their place.

Through trials faced, the heart grows wise,
In stillness, strength begins to rise.
With patience taught by every tear,
The soul restores, the path is clear.

So in the stillness, take your time,
In every breath, a rhythm's rhyme.
Embrace the quiet, let it fill,
For in the stillness, we heal.

## **Tides of Redemption**

In the stillness, faith takes flight,
Waves of grace wash sin from sight.
Hearts once heavy, now embrace,
The tender touch of Heaven's grace.

With every ebb, a chance to heal,
The sorrowed soul begins to feel.
A whisper found in ocean's roar,
Redemption calls, forevermore.

Through trials deep, we find our way,
Guided by the light of day.
Every stumble, every fall,
Is but a step toward love's great call.

Lifted high on faith's strong tide,
In His mercy, we abide.
Together bound by sacred ties,
In every heart, His love replies.

## Echoes of the Broken

Here in shadows, voices weep,
In the darkness, pain runs deep.
Yet in sorrow, hope can rise,
As faith unveils the brightened skies.

Battered souls, they seek the light,
In the midst of endless night.
Every echo sings a hymn,
Of strength reborn when hope seems dim.

Hands outstretched, forgive the past,
In love's embrace, our scars can last.
United hearts can build anew,
From brokenness, His mercy true.

In the silence, prayers ascend,
For healing hands that only mend.
Amidst the ruins, peace shall bloom,
As echoes guide us from the gloom.

## Pathways to Peace

Beneath the skies where angels tread,
A whispered promise gently said.
Each step we take, a path unfolds,
In quiet trust, our spirit holds.

With every dawn, the light restores,
A canvas blank, we paint with shores.
Guided by stars, a noble quest,
To find the peace within our chest.

Through valleys low, we walk with grace,
In faith we find our resting place.
With every trial, love will soar,
Creating bridges evermore.

In unity, we stand as one,
Together seeking what's begun.
As pathways lead to love's embrace,
In harmony, we find our space.

# **From Ashes We Rise**

From the ashes, hope is born,
In the twilight of the morn.
Every heart, like phoenix wings,
Soars above the pain life brings.

In the fire, a spirit gleams,
Woven deep in faith's great dreams.
Through the struggle, courage grows,
With every trial, true strength shows.

Break the chains that bind the soul,
In unity, we find the whole.
From shadows long, we seek the sun,
In love's embrace, we all are one.

With raised voices, we will sing,
To the hope that resurrection brings.
Through the journey, a path ignites,
From ashes bright, our spirit lights.

## Illuminated by Grace

In shadows deep, a light does gleam,
A whisper soft, a holy dream.
With open hearts, we seek the way,
Guided by love, we trust and pray.

The morning sun breaks through the night,
Each soul reborn, a precious sight.
With grace bestowed, we rise and stand,
Together strong, in faith, our hand.

Angels sing in harmony,
A chorus loud, we feel so free.
In every trial, His voice we find,
A gentle touch, our hearts aligned.

Through valleys low, we walk in peace,
With every step, our worries cease.
In trust we find our paths embrace,
Our journeys blessed, illuminated grace.

## **The Bridge to Tomorrow**

On troubled waters, faith shall rise,
A bridge of hope beneath the skies.
We walk with courage, hand in hand,
Towards horizons, bright and grand.

With every heartbeat, dreams take flight,
Together we shall face the night.
A promise made, our spirits soar,
In unity, we seek for more.

The past behind, we leave no mark,
For in His love, we find our spark.
Through trials faced, our strength will grow,
A shining path, His grace will show.

As dawn breaks forth, the day anew,
We look to Him, in all we do.
The bridge we build, of faith and grace,
Will guide us on, through time and space.

## Navigating the Depths

In silent waters, deep and wide,
We seek the truth, with love as guide.
In darkest hours, His light we see,
A beacon bright, eternally.

Each wave we ride, through storm and calm,
His whispered words, a soothing balm.
Through tempests fierce, our hearts stay true,
In every tide, we trust anew.

With faith as anchor, hope our sail,
Together strong, we shall prevail.
Through trials faced and lessons learned,
Our spirits grow, our souls discerned.

In depths of night, His love surrounds,
With every breath, our joy abounds.
We journey forth, in peace we find,
Navigating depths, by grace aligned.

## **The Language of Forgiveness**

In whispers soft, a heart's request,
We seek to heal, to love, to bless.
With every word, a chance to mend,
In forgiveness, we find a friend.

The burdens lifted, weight released,
In open arms, our souls find peace.
We share the grace that we've received,
In every heart, a love believed.

Through trials faced, we learn to grow,
In every hurt, compassion flows.
With open hearts, we break the chains,
In unity, love reclaims.

With every act, a bridge we build,
In kindness shown, our spirits filled.
In the language of forgiveness, we,
Bind wounds of old, and set souls free.

## Healing Whisper of Grace

In silence, grace speaks sweetly here,
A soft embrace that calms our fear.
With tender hands, the broken mend,
A whispered hope, a faithful friend.

The heart that aches, finds peace within,
As gentle winds sweep past our sin.
In every tear, a promise blooms,
Restoring life, dispelling gloom.

The light of dawn breaks cancer's hold,
In warmth of love, our hearts unfold.
In quiet moments, faith ignites,
A healing whisper through the nights.

With every breath, we rise anew,
Embracing all that's pure and true.
Our burdens shared, we find our space,
In every struggle, healing grace.

So trust the path our spirits take,
For in the trials, joy will wake.
With open hearts, the journey starts,
In healing whispers, grace imparts.

# Redemption's Light from Shadows

In shadows deep, a light will glow,
A guiding hand through pain and woe.
From brokenness, a song will rise,
Redemption waits beneath the skies.

With every step, the past released,
A banquet set, our doubts decreased.
In whispered prayers, our hearts unite,
Embracing love, redemption's light.

Through trials faced, our spirits soar,
A tapestry of grace we store.
With each new dawn, our faith ignites,
In shadows cast, we find our rights.

The chains that bind will fall away,
As love transforms, we learn to stay.
In every heart, a spark will blaze,
Redeeming souls in endless praise.

So lift your eyes, behold the dawn,
From shadows past, a heart reborn.
In every struggle, truth will shout,
Redemption's light will lead us out.

## Songs of the Overcomer

In battles fought, we raise our song,
A melody where we belong.
From ashes rise, our voices blend,
The songs of hope that never end.

Through storms we stand, unwavering,
In faith, we find what grace can bring.
With every trial, a note of praise,
The overcomer's strength displays.

In darkest nights, we find the spark,
A rhythm bright dispels the dark.
With every chord, our hearts awake,
In unity, our fears we shake.

With open arms, we share our story,
In every loss, behold His glory.
The songs of us, in harmony,
Echoing through eternity.

So sing aloud, let the heavens hear,
For in His love, we have no fear.
The songs we sing, a gift bestowed,
The overcomer's path is road.

## **Beneath the Weight of Sorrow**

Beneath the weight of sorrow deep,
In quiet moments, we shall weep.
Yet through the tears, a promise glows,
In pain, the seed of healing grows.

In valleys low, where shadows play,
Our hearts will seek the light of day.
With gentle hands, the hurt will mend,
And through the night, we find a friend.

The burdens shared with faithful grace,
Will lead us to a safer place.
In every storm, a shelter waits,
To guide us through these heavy gates.

In every sorrow, love's refrain,
Reminds us of the joy in pain.
For in each loss, a gain shall rise,
A deeper faith beyond the skies.

So lift your heart and let it be,
In sorrow's grip, we learn to see.
The beauty found in moments spent,
Beneath the weight, our hearts content.

## Beneath the Pillars of Grace

In the shadow of mercy, we tread soft,
With hearts uplifted, our spirits aloft.
Beneath the pillars, where faith stands tall,
Grace whispers gently, embracing us all.

Through trials we wander, yet love never fails,
In the light of His promise, hope ever sails.
Each step a reminder, we're never alone,
In the arms of our Savior, we find our home.

When storms bring their shadows, and darkness draws near,
His love is a beacon, quelling our fear.
With angels beside us, we rise above strife,
In the refuge of faith, we discover new life.

In moments of silence, where prayers take flight,
Our voices like candles, igniting the night.
For under His mercy, each soul finds its place,
In the boundless embrace, beneath pillars of grace.

So let us together, in unity stand,
With hearts full of gratitude, joined hand in hand.
For beneath the pillars, we cherish the space,
To love one another, beneath pillars of grace.

## **A Tapestry of Mercy**

Threads of compassion weave through the air,
In a tapestry vibrant, God's love laid bare.
Each stitch tells a story, of kindness bestowed,
In the fabric of mercy, our spirits are sowed.

Through valleys of shadows, the light brightly glows,
In the heart of the weary, true solace flows.
With every encounter, His kindness we share,
In a tapestry woven with exquisite care.

From strangers to family, His love does unite,
Each thread intertwined, in the darkest of night.
In the warmth of the woven, our burdens grow light,
For mercy surrounds us, a radiant sight.

As we gather our stories of trials and grace,
Each patch a reminder, no one's out of place.
From sorrow to joy, together we rise,
In a tapestry of mercy, the spirit complies.

So let love cover all, like a blanket of peace,
In a world that is longing, may kindness not cease.
For the tapestry glimmers, with hope we embrace,
In the art of compassion, we all find our place.

## **The Crossroads of Hope**

At twilight we gather, the path lies ahead,
The crossroads of hope, where all fears are shed.
Each sign points to promise, each turn a new way,
In the wisdom of stillness, our hearts learn to sway.

With faith as our compass, we're guided by light,
Every step taken, dispelling the night.
In the whispers of prayer, our spirits ascend,
At the crossroads of hope, where journeys transcend.

Through valleys of doubt, and mountains of grace,
We seek out the refuge that time can't erase.
In the arms of the Savior, our burdens released,
At the crossroads of hope, all our doubts find peace.

So let us remember, together we stand,
With dreams like the stars, as they scatter on land.
For at every intersection, love conquers fear,
In the crossroads of hope, we find what is dear.

With each new horizon, a chance to begin,
In unity spoken, we let light come in.
For the road may be winding, but together we cope,
At the junction of faith, we all find our hope.

## Flowers from Ruins

In the ashes of sorrow, new blossoms arise,
From ruins of heartache, a beauty defies.
With petals of courage, we stand in the sun,
For the flowers of hope have now just begun.

Through the cracks in our pain, life finds a way,
With colors of promise, transforming the gray.
Each fragrance a blessing, each bloom a sweet sign,
From ruins of yesterday, our spirits align.

In the garden of grace, we're nurtured and healed,
With love as our water, our wounds are revealed.
Though the storms may have battered, our hearts rediscover,
In the flowers of hope, we bloom for each other.

So let us be gardens, where kindness can grow,
In the soil of compassion, let resilience flow.
From the shattered remains, we rise and compose,
For in flowers from ruins, true beauty bestows.

With each tender blossom, our stories unfold,
In the warmth of connection, like sunlight we hold.
From the depths of despair, we rise to embrace,
The promise of tomorrow, in flowers from grace.

## Beneath the Old Oak

Beneath the old oak's mighty shade,
We gather in the balm of grace.
Whispers of hope in silence laid,
In God's embrace, we find our place.

The roots run deep, a sacred bond,
In every leaf, His mercy speaks.
We walk the path our hearts respond,
To love that comforts, heals the weak.

When storms arise, and shadows fall,
We stand as one, with faith unshaken.
His gentle call, our guiding thrall,
In trials faced, our fears forsaken.

The harvest time will surely come,
In fields of gold, our dreams will gleam.
With every prayer, the heartbeats drum,
Beneath the oak, we weave our dream.

Together here, we sing aloud,
In unity, our spirits soar.
Beneath the watch of heaven's cloud,
We find our strength forevermore.

## The Power of Unseen Hands

In the quiet hour, unseen hands,
Guide us through the darkest night.
Like gentle waves upon the sands,
They cradle us, till dawn brings light.

When burdens weigh, and hearts grow tired,
We seek the strength that lies within.
By faith alone, our souls are fired,
In grace, our struggles softly spin.

The mighty mountains bow to grace,
As storms of doubt begin to cease.
With every tear, God lights the space,
Transforming pain to lasting peace.

As whispers lift from hearts in prayer,
Each soul embraced, each spirit blessed.
In every moment, love laid bare,
The unseen hands bring hope's sweet rest.

In silent trust, we learn to stand,
In harmony, our spirits dance.
For in the grace of unseen hands,
We find the joy of happenstance.

# Faith's Gentle Caress

In the stillness of the dawn,
Faith whispers softly, sweet and clear.
A tender grace that's gently drawn,
To cradle us throughout the year.

Through trials faced, our hearts may ache,
With every step, we're not alone.
The path of love, for love's own sake,
Another day, our hopes have grown.

The light of truth will guide our way,
In shadows cast, it shines so bright.
In storms of life, He will not sway,
Faith's gentle caress brings us light.

Be still, my soul, let troubles cease,
In prayer, we find the strength to rise.
Through every doubt, we seek His peace,
Embraced within the love that ties.

As blossoms bloom in seasons' change,
We journey forth with hearts in bloom.
With faith as roots, we shall not range,
In love divine, we find our room.

## **The Tapestry of Our Trials**

Threads of sorrow weave with light,
In the tapestry of our days.
Each struggle faced, a piece of might,
In colors bold, through life's arrays.

With every stitch, a lesson learned,
In joy and grief, we find our way.
The fabric of our hearts has turned,
With grace to guide, come what may.

In trials deep, our strength is born,
Through faith, the needle finds a path.
From darkest nights, the hope is worn,
In woven dreams, we share the wrath.

Together here, we stand as one,
Each thread a story, rich and true.
In God's design, our battles won,
Unified in all we do.

So let our lives, a tapestry,
Of love and faith, forever thread.
A testament of unity,
In every word and prayer we've said.

## Mysteries of the Soul

In the silence deep and pure,
Whispers of the heart endure,
Veils of night and light entwined,
Secrets of the soul we find.

Faith like rivers flowing wide,
Guides us through the worldly tide,
In the shadows, grace unfolds,
Stories of the brave and bold.

Echoes of a voice divine,
Call us to the sacred line,
Through the trials, we ascend,
In His arms, we find our friend.

Every tear that falls in prayer,
Meets the love that's always there,
In the depths of darkest night,
We emerge into the light.

Journey on through endless time,
Trusting in the heart's sweet rhyme,
Each mystery, a path we tread,
In the light, our fears are shed.

## **Stones of Remembrance**

Upon the hill where shadows lay,
Stones speak of a brighter day,
Each one holds a story true,
Of the old, and of the new.

Chiseled words of hope and grace,
Echo softly in this space,
Whispers of the ones who prayed,
In the night when light had strayed.

Gathered here with faith as guide,
Every heart that's opened wide,
Marks of love engraved in time,
Testimony in every chime.

From ashes rise a sacred song,
In remembrance, we belong,
With every stone, our spirits soar,
United in the search for more.

Through valleys low and mountains high,
We lift our gaze beyond the sky,
Trusting stones will ever speak,
Of divine strength in the weak.

# The Cry of Redemption

In the depths of anguish loud,
A voice calls from the shrouded crowd,
With each heartache, every fall,
The cry of redemption, hear the call.

Through the darkness, a beacon shines,
Hope reforged in sacred lines,
Forgiveness flows as rivers wide,
In the bonds of love, we abide.

Lifted hands and humble pleas,
Gather strength upon the knees,
In the struggle, we are blessed,
In His mercy, find our rest.

Every sin a heavy chain,
Broken, we rise free from pain,
In the light of grace restored,
Every soul by Love adored.

In the hush of midnight's grace,
Feel the warmth of His embrace,
For in every tear we find,
A promise, gentle and kind.

## **The Serpent and the Dove**

In the garden where shadows play,
The serpent whispers, leads astray,
Yet from the heights, a dove descends,
Bringing peace that never ends.

Amid the chaos, choices bloom,
Life and death within the room,
Each decision, sacred ground,
In love's embrace, hope is found.

Wisdom dances with the meek,
In every heart, the spirit speaks,
Trials faced with faith as shield,
In surrender, souls are healed.

As the serpent coils and strikes,
The dove rises with gentle might,
In the struggle, truth will reign,
Uniting joy within our pain.

Through the shadows, light will guide,
In the Lord, we shall abide,
For every serpent, we are wise,
With doves of love that never die.

## Whispers of the Untamed Spirit

In the quiet night, spirits sigh,
A breeze carries prayers to the sky.
Stars twinkle bright with ancient grace,
Guiding the lost in this vast space.

Echoes of faith in the rustling leaves,
A dance of hope that never weaves.
Each heartbeat whispers, a deep refrain,
In the wilderness, love will remain.

Nature sings softly, a sacred song,
Drawing the weary to where they belong.
Through valleys of doubt, the spirit roams,
Finding its way in the heart's unknown.

Mountains stand tall, revealing truth,
Their silent witness to life's pure youth.
In every shadow, a light is found,
The untamed spirit, forever unbound.

So listen closely to nature's call,
In the wild depths, we rise, we fall.
Together we journey, hand in hand,
In whispers of truth, we understand.

## A Celestial Mosaic

In the tapestry of the night sky,
Stars like jewels begin to cry.
Each twinkle tells of a prayer sent,
A celestial mosaic, heaven's intent.

Clouds drift softly, carrying dreams,
Beneath their shadows, the heart redeems.
The moonlight whispers truths untold,
In silver beams, our hopes unfold.

Fractal galaxies spin with grace,
In their depths, we find our place.
A harmony of souls that intertwine,
Dancing together by cosmic design.

With every sunrise, colors ignite,
Painting the world with love and light.
In this artistry, we find our role,
As pieces of beauty, we touch the whole.

So gaze upon wonders woven tight,
In the vast expanse, we see the light.
Together we chant in unity's name,
Whispers of love, we rise, we claim.

# **The Prayer of the Wounded**

In shadows deep, the wounded lie,
With aching hearts that long to cry.
They seek the balm of a gentle hand,
To heal the sorrows no one can understand.

Tears like rivers flow down their cheeks,
A silent language in hope it speaks.
In pain, they find a fragile grace,
A prayer hung softly in this lonely space.

O, bring your light to those who mourn,
In the silence, let compassion be born.
Through every heart that beats with fear,
May love's embrace draw near, so near.

For in each wound lies strength divine,
A chance to mend, a thread to intertwine.
With every heartbeat, let healing start,
Together we gather, one broken heart.

So here we cultivate a sacred ground,
Where in our sorrow, love is found.
The prayer of the wounded softly hums,
In unity's solace, redemption comes.

## **Blossoms from Brokenness**

From shattered dreams, new life can rise,
A testament to the strength inside.
In barren soil, seeds of hope are sown,
Blossoms from brokenness are gently grown.

With every fracture, the light shines through,
Creating patterns in vibrant hues.
Each petal speaks of a story shared,
Of love that flourished when it was dared.

In the embrace of the gentle rain,
Healing begins to break the chain.
Roots entwined in the heart's warm earth,
Finding joy in the midst of hurt.

So let us nurture what pain has taught,
The beauty that struggles have wrought.
In every bloom, a soul reborn,
From the ashes, eternal light is worn.

Together we rise, hand in hand,
Celebrating life, both fragile and grand.
For in every ending, a new tale calls,
Blossoms from brokenness, love never falls.

## **Souls Alight in the Darkness**

In shadows deep, where whispers dwell,
Our spirits rise, the night to quell.
With candles bright, we seek the light,
In unity, we forge our flight.

Hearts ablaze, in faith we stand,
Together strong, we lend a hand.
Through trials faced, our love will guide,
In every tear, His truth resides.

From ashes cold, we find our way,
In silent prayers, our souls shall sway.
Each step we take, the path unfolds,
In grace embraced, our faith enfolds.

A tapestry of stars above,
We gather hopes, we weave with love.
In darkest nights, our spirits sing,
With lifted hearts, our praises ring.

For every wound, a healing song,
In sacred bonds, we all belong.
With every breath, this promise dear,
In love divine, we have no fear.

## **Labyrinths of Grace**

In winding paths, our journey flows,
Through twists and turns, the spirit grows.
Each corner turned, reveals anew,
The love that binds, the heart so true.

With every prayer, a lantern bright,
Guides weary souls through endless night.
In solitude, we find our peace,
As grace envelops, doubts release.

In gentle whispers, wisdom speaks,
Through valleys low, and mountain peaks.
The map of faith, etched deep within,
Leads us forth, where hope begins.

With faith as guide, we journey on,
Through thorny paths, we are reborn.
Each step we take, a sacred dance,
In trust we rise, in love's expanse.

Through labyrinths, our spirits soar,
With every trial, we seek out more.
In endless grace, we find our way,
In each embrace, we learn to stay.

## The Offering of Our Scars

In brokenness, a story told,
Of battles fought, and hearts of gold.
Each scar a mark, of love's embrace,
In every wound, we find His grace.

Our hands uplifted, we share our pain,
In unity, we break the chain.
With every tear, we build a bridge,
Through suffering, we honor His image.

These scars we bear, a testament,
To battles won, a life well-spent.
In tenderness, we find our way,
In every heart, His love will stay.

From darkness deep, His light shines bright,
Through shattered dreams, we find our sight.
In offering hearts, we rise again,
With scars adorned, we gather strength.

The pain we hold, becomes our song,
In every note, we all belong.
For every heart, a chance to heal,
Through love and scars, we learn to feel.

## **Rebirth Within the Storm**

Amidst the tempest, a whisper calls,
Through raging winds, our spirit falls.
In every trial, a chance to grow,
Within the storm, His love will flow.

Each lightning flash reveals the dawn,
In darkest hours, we are reborn.
Through thunder's roar, we find our voice,
In chaos fierce, we will rejoice.

The waves may crash, but we will stand,
United firm, hand in hand.
With every surge, we learn to trust,
In Him alone, our strength is just.

Through tempest's rage, our hearts ignite,
In faith we rise, from depths of night.
With every heartbeat, love's refrain,
In storms of life, we break the chain.

For in each storm, new life begins,
With every end, the Spirit sings.
In sacred cycles, we embrace,
With love reborn, we find our place.

# Reflections in the Water

In the stillness, a mirror lies,
Ripples dance 'neath the vast skies.
Each glimmer, a whisper of grace,
God's love shines bright in this sacred space.

When storms arise and shadows creep,
The water's depths hold secrets deep.
Beneath the surface, peace abides,
Trust in His hand, where hope resides.

The world may waver, and hearts may tire,
Yet in the calm, we find our fire.
A gentle rest in His sweet embrace,
Reflections guide us to His place.

With every droplet, a promise made,
In trials and storms, He will not fade.
The waters speak of love untold,
In every wave, His hand we hold.

So gaze upon the tranquil sea,
Let every ripple set you free.
In each reflection, a truth unfolds,
In God's own image, our heart He molds.

## Cast Your Burdens

When heavy hearts feel the weight,
In His presence, we find our fate.
Lay down your fears, release your pain,
In His mercy, we rise again.

With hands outstretched, the Savior waits,
To lighten loads, to open gates.
Through trials faced, we're not alone,
His love surrounds, we are His own.

In whispered prayers, our souls unite,
He hears each cry, brings forth the light.
From depths of sorrow, we shall soar,
He mends the heart and opens doors.

Cast burdens down, let grace abound,
In every loss, new hope is found.
The path may twist, yet He is near,
Awake your spirit, cast out fear.

For in surrender, we find our song,
In sweet release, we all belong.
So lift your eyes, the dawn is bright,
In faith, we stand, embraced by light.

# The Weight of Glory

A whisper calls from realms above,
To carry forth His dream of love.
In trials faced, we find our role,
Each burden shared, enriches the soul.

The weight we bear is not in vain,
In grief and sorrow, we grow through pain.
For every tear, a lesson learned,
In depths of night, our hearts are burned.

He beckons us to rise and stand,
With faith in heart, and open hand.
The glory formed through every fight,
Transforms our darkness into light.

Through valleys deep, we walk with grace,
His presence shines, a warm embrace.
In every struggle, the spirit glows,
The weight of glory, as love bestows.

So journey on with heads held high,
In unity, let our spirits fly.
For through our trials, He covers us,
In Him alone, our hearts will trust.

## **Blossoming After the Storm**

In shadows cast by tempest's might,
New blooms arise, embracing light.
The storms may rage, the winds may howl,
Yet beauty whispers, soft as an owl.

With raindrops' touch, the earth revives,
In trials faced, true strength derives.
Each petal unfolds, a story shared,
Of love and grace, that He has bared.

Through seasons changing, we find our tune,
The sun breaks forth, a smiling moon.
From brokenness, a new song sings,
In faith and hope, our spirit springs.

For every storm that comes our way,
Brings forth new life, brightens each day.
In every heart, a seed is sown,
To blossom forth, our faith has grown.

So let the winds blow, let the rain pour,
For in our hearts, love will restore.
Through trials faced, and pain endured,
In His embrace, our hope is assured.

## **Embracing the Divine Narrative**

In the sacred story, we find our place,
Threads of faith woven in eternal grace.
Every heart whispers, each soul is a song,
Together we travel, where we all belong.

Through trials and triumphs, wisdom unfolds,
Ancient truths echo, a tale that is told.
In shadows and light, we seek the embrace,
Of love that transcends, of boundless space.

With eyes set on heavens, we witness the dawn,
Each moment of stillness, a promise reborn.
From ashes to beauty, in prayer we ascend,
In the sacred narrative, we meet our true friend.

In whispers of scripture, our spirits take flight,
Guided by grace, we step into the light.
The chorus of ages harmonizes here,
A symphony vibrant, dispelling all fear.

So let us unite in the stories we weave,
Embracing the journey, in love we believe.
The divine narrative, our hearts will ignite,
In the temple of life, we walk with delight.

## The Threshing Floor of Renewal

Upon the threshing floor, we lay it all down,
Grain of our burdens, trampled by crown.
In surrender, we gather, our faith intertwined,
From chaos to clarity, true peace we find.

With every heartbeat, we feel the release,
As winds of the Spirit bring whispers of peace.
In the dance of the chaff, may our spirits rise,
Cleansed in the presence, dressed in the skies.

The light of redemption breaks forth in the dust,
Through trials and heartaches, in Him we trust.
With joy as our harvest, we reap what we've sown,
A testament blooming, through love we have grown.

Who can measure the bounty, the grace overflowed?
In the furnace of love, our hearts are bestowed.
Through seasons of waiting, new life shall emerge,
On this threshing floor, our souls gently surge.

So let us rejoice, let our praises be known,
For in every struggle, His mercy is shown.
The threshing floor calls, let us answer in faith,
For renewal is coming, through love we embrace.

## Hands Lifted in Gratitude

Hands lifted high, we come to adore,
With hearts full of thanks, as we seek evermore.
In moments of silence, we feel the divine,
Interwoven with blessings, His light ever shines.

Every breath is a whisper, a gift from above,
In the arms of the Father, we feel His great love.
With gratitude flowing, we stand side by side,
In the warmth of His presence, we find our true guide.

The stars in the heavens reflect His embrace,
Through trials and triumphs, we run this race.
With hands raised in praise, we echo His name,
In humility's beauty, we welcome the flame.

From mountains to valleys, our voices unite,
A chorus of love, through darkness and light.
With hearts wide open, we share in His grace,
In joy and in sorrow, we seek His face.

So let us come together, in reverent cheer,
With hands lifted high, our spirits sincere.
For gratitude's song is a hymn to the skies,
In the arms of the Savior, our hopes ever rise.

## **Holiness Among the Shattered**

In the fragments of life, His glory still shines,
Among the broken hearts, His love intertwines.
Through every sorrow, a sacred embrace,
In the tears and the trials, we find our true grace.

The shattered remain, yet beauty can bloom,
From ashes to hope, dispelling the gloom.
In faith's gentle whisper, we gather the pieces,
For holiness rises, and darkness ceases.

With each act of kindness, we stitch up the seams,
In the fabric of love, we weave our dreams.
In the depths of despair, His light will appear,
A guide to the weary, a refuge sincere.

So let us walk forward, hand in hand, we stand,
In the midst of the shattered, He leads, ever grand.
With grace as our armor, our hearts clarified,
Holiness among us, with arms opened wide.

In the brokenness shared, new life can begin,
For in each of our stories, His presence within.
We rise through our cracks, like the dawn's early light,
Holiness found in the depths of the night.

## **Yielding to the Divine**

In silence, I kneel, seeking grace,
Your whispers surround me, a warm embrace.
Each doubt fades like shadows at noon,
In the light of Your love, I am in tune.

With every heartbeat, I offer my all,
In faith, I rise, though I often fall.
The path may twist, but I'll trust the way,
For Your guiding hand shall never stray.

Oh, mercy flows like rivers wide,
In trials and troubles, You're by my side.
When burdens weigh and hope seems thin,
A whisper of peace invites me within.

The mountains may roar, the seas may churn,
In this vast world, it's Your wisdom I yearn.
With every breath, I surrender my will,
In the presence of love, my heart is still.

So here I stand, at the altar of life,
In moments of joy and times of strife.
With every prayer, I find my voice,
In yielding to You, I rejoice.

## Wings of the Heart

Upon the winds of faith I soar,
Carried by love, forevermore.
Each gentle breeze whispers Your name,
In flight, I find my soul's true aim.

With every tear, a lesson learned,
Through trials faced, my spirit burned.
In shadows cast, Your light will lead,
A beacon bright in every need.

Oh, lift me high, beyond the fray,
On wings of hope, guide me each day.
Through valleys low and skies so wide,
In trust, I journey, with You as my guide.

The world may tremble, the skies may weep,
Yet in Your arms, I long to keep.
Each fluttering heart, a song to sing,
In unity, we rise on love's bright wing.

So let me soar, unhindered, free,
In every heartbeat, there lies a decree.
Embracing life, with each new start,
I take to the skies, on wings of the heart.

## The Promise of Dawn

As night recedes, the shadows flee,
With every sunrise, You're close to me.
In colors bold, the sky does glow,
A testament of love that's pure as snow.

The promise of dawn casts fears aside,
With each golden ray, our spirits glide.
Through tears and laughter, life flows sweet,
In the embrace of morning, we meet.

Oh, dawn arises, gentle and kind,
In Your embrace, new strength I find.
Each day unfolds with hope anew,
In faith, I rise, my heart entwined with You.

Across the heavens, hymns do soar,
In gratitude, my soul I pour.
For every promise, I hold dear,
In the warmth of the dawn, I draw near.

Let me walk forth, with heart ablaze,
In the splendor of life, I sing Your praise.
For the promise of dawn, I ever yearn,
In every moment, Your love I discern.

## A Psalm for Every Tear

In the depths of sorrow, I find my song,
Each tear a note, where I belong.
In moments heavy, when darkness lingers,
I raise my hands and feel Your fingers.

Oh, hear my cry, in depths unknown,
In every heartbeat, I am not alone.
For in each trial, a psalm does rise,
A melody of hope beneath the skies.

Through valleys low, my spirit weeps,
Yet in Your arms, my heart still keeps.
A rhythm formed from pain and grace,
In every tear, I see Your face.

So let me sing, though shadows fall,
For in Your presence, I'll heed the call.
Each tear a testament, a sacred spark,
In this journey bright, through light and dark.

Each psalm I write, a testament true,
With every sorrow, I draw to You.
In the embrace of faith, my spirit will steer,
For there's a psalm for every tear.

## Hallowed Ground of Memory

In whispers soft, the past unfolds,
Where sacred tales of love retold.
On hallowed ground, our souls align,
In every heart, a trace divine.

Beneath the stars, our hopes arise,
In solemn nights, we seek the skies.
Each memory, a sacred thread,
A guiding light, where angels tread.

Through shadows cast by time's embrace,
We find our peace, our sacred space.
In moments past, forever bright,
Our spirits soar, transcending night.

The echoes call, the voices blend,
In every heart, a chance to mend.
With every breath, the truth we seek,
In silence deep, the heavens speak.

Thus let us walk on paths serene,
In hallowed ground where we convene.
Together bound, we rise anew,
In memory's heart, we find what's true.

## Sanctum of the Spirit

In quietude, the spirit sighs,
A sacred space where love complies.
Within the walls of grace we dwell,
In whispers soft, our hearts rebel.

The light within, a flickering flame,
In every soul, a holy name.
With every prayer, the bond we weave,
In faith's embrace, we dare believe.

Through trials faced and burdens borne,
In unity, a new day's dawn.
The sanctum holds our silent cries,
Each tear a jewel, a spirit rise.

In sacred halls where thoughts ascend,
The love we share, a timeless blend.
In every heart, a peace restored,
In every glance, a soul adored.

Thus let us gather, hand in hand,
In sanctum's light, forever stand.
With heart aglow, we sing our way,
In spirit's dance, we choose to stay.

**Wounds Like Prayer**

In tender hearts, the wounds we bear,
A silent plea, a whispered prayer.
Through cracks of pain, the light streams in,
In every scar, a chance to win.

With every tear, a story flows,
In darkness deep, the spirit grows.
Each wound like prayer, a bridge of trust,
In healing grace, we rise from dust.

Embracing light that filters down,
In humble hearts, we wear a crown.
For every trial, a lesson learned,
In wounds like prayer, our spirits turned.

Let love arise from pain and loss,
In faith's embrace, we bear the cross.
For every hurt, a hope reborn,
In wounds like prayer, our souls adorned.

Thus with each step, we pave the way,
In love and light, forever stay.
Embracing all that life may send,
In wounds like prayer, we find our friends.

## **Embracing the Light**

In dawn's embrace, the shadows flee,
With every breath, we long to see.
A radiant glow, the spirit shines,
In every heart, a love aligns.

Through valleys deep and mountains high,
We seek the truth beyond the sky.
In every trial, we feel the grace,
Embracing light, our sacred space.

With faith ablaze, we rise as one,
In unity, our journey's begun.
Each step we take, a dance divine,
In countless hearts, our souls entwine.

Thus let us walk on paths of gold,
In stories shared, our hearts unfold.
With every dawn, a chance to grow,
Embracing light, our spirits glow.

In harmony, our voices rise,
To meet the challenge, reach the skies.
In every moment, a gift we find,
Embracing the light, forever kind.

## **Finding Solace in Silence**

In the stillness where shadows dance,
Whispers of peace begin to prance.
Hearts aligned in quiet grace,
In silence, we find our sacred space.

Bathed in light, the soul takes flight,
Soft echoes break the night.
Here in silence, burdens cease,
In the heart, we find our peace.

From turmoil's grasp, we gently part,
With open arms, we hear the heart.
In solitude, we lay our fears,
And find the strength to dry our tears.

Each breath, a gift, a chance to be,
In the silence, we become free.
Listening close to the essence within,
In the hush, our journey begins.

As the stars grace the endless night,
We embrace the calm, the divine light.
In the silence, love will reveal,
A sacred truth that we can feel.

## Through the Valley of Light

In valleys green, where shadows fade,
The light unfolds, a promise made.
Upon the path, our spirits soar,
With faith as armor, we seek more.

Through every trial, we walk as one,
Guided by grace, until it's done.
In the valley, hope ignites,
A flicker shining through the nights.

With each step, the burden eases,
In sacred spaces, the soul pleases.
The dawn breaks bright, a gentle call,
In light's embrace, we shall not fall.

Every echo a loving song,
In unity, where we belong.
Through valleys low, our spirits climb,
Together weaving love and rhyme.

So hold the light within your sight,
For every shadow yields to light.
In the valley, we find our way,
Embracing love, come what may.

## **Banners of Faith**

We raise our banners, bold and true,
In colors bright, the journey's hue.
With hearts united, we stand strong,
In faith's embrace, we're never wrong.

Through storm and strife, we hold our ground,
In sacred words, our hope is found.
In every cry, in every prayer,
The banners wave, we are aware.

Together we rise, through trials faced,
In love's sweet light, our fears erased.
With every step, we carry on,
Banners of faith, until the dawn.

Let courage fill our weary minds,
With faith as compass, love binds.
In the darkest night, we shine bright,
Our spirits lead, in purest light.

So lift your voice and sing aloud,
In hope's embrace, we are proud.
For in this journey, we find grace,
Banners of faith, our warm embrace.

## **Prayerful Whispers**

In moments hushed, the heart can speak,
With whispered prayers, we seek the meek.
Each word a thread in sacred bliss,
In prayerful whispers, we find our kiss.

Through gentle sighs, our worries flow,
To realms where love and grace will grow.
In stillness, the Holy breathes,
As joyful hearts weave tender wreaths.

From depths of soul, our hopes arise,
As clouds disperse, revealing skies.
In every whisper, power lies,
With faith as wings, our spirit flies.

Together, we gather, hearts entwined,
In prayerful whispers, we are aligned.
A chorus sweet, we blend and weave,
In daily grace, we all believe.

So speak your truth in softest tones,
For in these whispers, love is known.
In prayerful moments, our souls ignite,
Guided by faith, we embrace the light.

## **Sacred Echoes of Resilience**

In the silence, prayers arise,
Whispers of courage in the skies.
Hearts entwined, we stand as one,
Beneath the warmth of sacred sun.

Through storms that shake our very ground,
Faithful spirits know no bound.
With every step, we rise, we soar,
In sacred echoes, we hear the roar.

Guided by light from heavens above,
We find our strength in endless love.
No trial too great to withstand,
In unity, we take our stand.

With hope's bright flame that never fades,
We walk through dark and endless shades.
In the tapestry of life we weave,
Together, stronger, we believe.

Each heartbeat sings, a life reborn,
From ashes rises, hope adorned.
In sacred spaces, souls ignite,
Resilience blooms, a radiant light.

## **Embracing the Divine Embrace**

In quiet stillness, grace unfolds,
Tender hands, a warmth that holds.
Wrapped in love, divine and pure,
Our spirits dance, the heart's allure.

Through valleys deep and mountains high,
We seek the truth beneath the sky.
In every tear, a lesson flows,
A gentle touch, compassion grows.

In shadows cast, we find our way,
With faith's embrace, we face the day.
Each moment shared, a sacred thread,
In divine love, our fears are shed.

The warmth of mercy fills the air,
With open hearts, we learn to care.
In unity, we rise as one,
Embraced by grace, our journey's begun.

In every heartbeat, presence felt,
A symphony of love, so heartfelt.
Through trials faced, we gently sway,
In divine embrace, we'll find our way.

# Through the Veil of Tears

In sorrow's grasp, we seek the light,
Each tear that falls, a shining bright.
Through heavy clouds, our spirits soar,
In the storm's embrace, we learn to endure.

With every loss, our hearts expand,
In the silence, we understand.
Each moment grief begins to fade,
In the depths, new hopes are laid.

The veil of tears, a sacred place,
Where broken hearts find their grace.
In whispered prayers, we find our strength,
Through pain we grow, at every length.

In shadows deep, the light will shine,
As love's embrace begins to align.
With faith, we rise from what we've known,
Through the veil, our seeds are sown.

From sorrow's grip, new dreams take flight,
In every struggle, we find delight.
Through the veil of tears, we pave the way,
Towards brighter tomorrows, come what may.

## **The Light that Follows**

In darkest nights, a beacon glows,
The path ahead, a light that shows.
With every step, our faith ignites,
Guided by love, through endless nights.

Upon the winds, a voice we hear,
In gentle whispers, calm our fear.
Through trials faced, we learn to grow,
The light that follows helps us know.

In every heart, a spark resides,
Illuminating, where hope abides.
Through valleys low and mountains steep,
In the light, our dreams we keep.

With open arms, we greet the dawn,
A symphony of life reborn.
In every shadow, courage thrives,
The light that follows, forever drives.

In unity, our spirits rise,
Together, we paint across the skies.
With love as our guide, we walk the way,
The light that follows, our hearts display.

## Gathering Broken Pieces

In the shadow of sorrow, we stand,
Collecting fragments of the heart's land.
Each shard a story, a moment lost,
We weave them gently, no matter the cost.

From pain's embrace, we rise anew,
Together in faith, we'll find what's true.
A tapestry stitched with love so vast,
In brokenness, find strength to last.

The light of hope flickers bright,
Guiding us through the darkest night.
With every piece, a promise made,
In unity, our fears will fade.

Hand in hand, we shall mend,
With grace and compassion, our hearts ascend.
We gather the pieces, one by one,
In the warmth of love, we become as one.

So let us gather, let us heal,
In the sacred space, our wounds conceal.
For in the broken, beauty is found,
In the gathering, love's voice resounds.

## A Path to Redemption

Upon the road of trials we walk,
With heavy hearts, we learn to talk.
Each step a struggle, yet grace appears,
In the silence, we confront our fears.

We seek forgiveness, a gentle call,
To rise above and not to fall.
In shadows deep, His light breaks through,
A path to redemption, bright and true.

The journey is long, yet worth the strife,
Reviving the spirit, breathing life.
With every stumble, we find our ground,
In love's embrace, our souls unbound.

The steps of mercy lead us near,
To the heart of the One who hears.
In humility, we lay our past,
On the altar of love, our shadows cast.

A new beginning, each dawn a sign,
In repentance, we align,
With every heartbeat, grace bestowed,
On this sacred path, our burdensode.

## The Divine Palette of Healing

In the artist's hand, colors collide,
Each hue a whisper, where hearts abide.
Brushstrokes of love paint the soul bright,
Transforming the darkness back into light.

With patience, He layers each shade,
Healing the wounds that time has made.
A palette rich with lessons learned,
In the fires of suffering, our spirits burned.

Every sorrow, a canvas anew,
Each tear a stroke, creating what's true.
In suffering, beauty begins to form,
The art of redemption through every storm.

Let the colors blend and embrace,
In diversity, we find our place.
The masterpiece rises, both rough and sweet,
In the Divine's hands, our hearts' heartbeat.

Thus let us trust in the grand design,
The art of healing, a love divine.
For in every broken piece of art,
Lies a story of grace, a new start.

## In the Arms of Mercy

In the stillness of night, we find our peace,
In the arms of mercy, all troubles cease.
Cradled in love, we softly weep,
For every promise, His heart will keep.

With tender grace, He holds us near,
Whispering truth, calming our fear.
In moments of doubt, His voice a guide,
In faith's embrace, we shall abide.

When the weight of the world feels too much,
His gentle presence, a sacred touch.
In the arms of mercy, we are reborn,
Through trials faced, a spirit worn.

Let burdens be laid at His feet,
For in His mercy, we are complete.
Each heartbeat a rhythm, a song divine,
In the embrace of love, our spirits shine.

So let us journey, hand in hand,
In the arms of mercy, forever we'll stand.
With compassion and hope, we'll carry forth,
To a land of grace, a new birth's worth.

Milton Keynes UK
Ingram Content Group UK Ltd.
UKHW031321271124
451618UK00007B/164